D0929525

The ABCs of LSU

The ABCs of LSU

Text by Linda Colquitt Taylor

Illustrations by Erin Casteel

Louisiana State University Press

Baton Rouge

Published by Louisiana State University Press
Text copyright © 2020 by Linda Colquitt Taylor
Illustrations copyright © 2020 by Erin Casteel
All rights reserved
Manufactured in the United States of America
First printing

Designer: Michelle A. Neustrom
Typeface: Tobi Pro
Printer and binder: Josten's

Library of Congress Cataloging-in-Publication Data

Names: Taylor, Linda Colquitt, author. | Casteel, Erin E. I., illustrator.
Title: The ABCs of LSU / text by Linda Colquitt Taylor ; illustrations by
    Erin Casteel.
Description: Baton Rouge : Louisiana State University Press, 2020. |
    Audience: Ages 4–8 | Audience: Grades K-1
Identifiers: LCCN 2019052543 | ISBN 978-0-8071-7387-9 (cloth)
Subjects: LCSH: Louisiana State University (Baton Rouge, La.)—Juvenile
    literature.
Classification: LCC LD3113 .T38 2020 | DDC 378.763/18—dc23
LC record available at https://lccn.loc.gov/2019052543

The paper in this book meets the guidelines for permanence and durability
of the Committee on Production Guidelines for Book Longevity of the Council
on Library Resources. ♾

In loving memory of my mother and father,
Ethel and Charles Colquitt of Shreveport,
Louisiana, both graduates of LSU.
They instilled in me a passion for the
university that I have in turn passed down
to my children and grandchildren.
Forever LSU!
—L.C.T.

Aa

Pete Maravich **A**ssembly Center waits for you,
An **A**rena for basketball and gymnastics too.
At **A**lex Box Stadium, "Home run!" fans scream.
Six national championships for the baseball team!

Bb

Baton Rouge, "Red Stick," LSU's home,
State capital, here we come!
Built on a **B**luff of the Mississippi River,
The flagship's campus education delivers.

Cc

From the **C**ampanile, or Memorial Tower,
Bells ring **C**learly on the hour.
Around the lakes are **C**ypress trees,
Gators might swim there, so be **C**areful please!

Dd

Tiger Band **D**rumline stops on Victory Hill.
Cymbals, snares, bass give us a thrill!
To the Ag Center **D**airy Store for a cold treat,
Delicious ice cream tasty and sweet.

Evangeline Hall where students sleep, work, and read.
Beds, lamps, desks, chairs are all that they need.
Egrets soar above LSU lakes.
White pelicans visit for winter breaks.

Ff

Free Speech Alley, where ideas get debated,
Opinions, beliefs, and Feelings are stated.
The French House was a Foreign language space,
Now the Ogden Honors College place.

Gg

Golden **G**irls step, dazzle, and shine,
Dance moves and kicks in a perfect line.
Greek Theater used to hold **G**raduation.
A new college degree means celebration!

Hh

Homecoming parade with a special theme.
At **H**alftime the crowning of king and queen.
The Cook **H**otel, to spend the night,
Sweet dreams until the morning light!

Ii

Italian-style buildings mighty and grand,
Tile roofs of red, stucco walls of tan.
Two hills called the **I**ndian Mounds.
Treat with care these ancient grounds.

Jj

T-33 Jet on display,
Stop on by and see it today!
Jazz students make an upbeat sound,
Trumpets, trombones, clarinets all around.

Kk

Tune to radio station **K**LSU,
Hear all **K**inds of music and campus news too.
First **K**ettle to boil sugar from cane,
Kept years outside through shine and rain.

Ll

Middleton **L**ibrary **L**ends books for **L**earning,
New information keeps pages turning.
Old **L**aw Building is stately and fine,
Like U.S. Supreme Court Building's design.

Mm

Mike the Tiger, hear his powerful roar!
Magnificent cat all the fans adore.
Museums of art and science too,
Exciting field trips at LSU!

Nn

LSU **N**ewspaper called *The Reveille,*
Students write articles and take pictures to see.
From the **N**orth Gate to **N**icholson Drive,
The latest **N**ews comes alive.

Oo

Memorial **O**ak Grove provides coolness and shade.
Under low-hanging branches, take a break in your day.
"**O**le War Skule" nickname from years long ago,
When student cadets drilled row by row.

Pp

"Love **P**urple Live Gold" stays true in our hearts,
Devotion to LSU never departs.
John M. **P**arker Coliseum hosts rodeos,
Nicknamed "Cow **P**alace" with livestock shows.

Qq

The four-sided **Q**uad, a **Q**uiet landscape,
With live oaks, azaleas, and myrtles of crepe.
Questions and answers in each classroom nearby,
Study hard for exams; the semester flies by!

Rr

Students take part in **R**OTC,
Army, navy, air force officers-to-be.
Reilly Theatre, a barn at first,
Now actors go there to perform and **R**ehearse.

Ss

Stadium echoes with the thunder of fans.
Something good to eat from the food **S**tands.
Many **S**teps to climb, row after row,
Scoreboards above, field below.

Tt

"**T**iger Bait" shouts on football game day,
Painted whiskers and noses on faces displayed.
"Hey Fightin' **T**igers! Fight all the way!
Play Fightin' **T**igers! Win the game today!"

Uu

Student **U**nion, a big place to study or eat,
Relax, pick up mail, wait to meet.
UREC, where fitness and exercise begin,
Run, swim, or climb, lift weights and spin.

Vv

Death **V**alley ready for Saturday night,
Visiting teams shake and tremble in fright.
Victory! LSU wins the game!
"Let's celebrate!" the team exclaims.

Ww

War Memorial on the Parade Ground,
Honored veterans gather round.
Wall with names of soldiers lost,
Freedom isn't free; there's always a cost.

Xx

Xylophone music delightful to hear,
Golden Band from Tigerland held so dear.
See the letter X on Sorority Row?
That's "chi" in Greek in case you don't know!

The Gumbo **Y**earbook, with many pictures inside
Showing students, events, and Tiger pride.
"We looked so **Y**oung!" alumni say,
"Decades ago seem like **Y**esterday!"

Zz

Zig-**Z**agging quarterback makes the pass,
Wide receiver catches, then runs fast.
Zero mistakes, no flags are thrown,
LSU's goal! We're in the end **Z**one!